POEMS

Portrait taken in Leipzig, 1910. (Yale Collection of American
Literature, Beinecke Rare Book and Manuscript Library)

CONTENTS

Introduction © 2002 by the Board of Trustees
of the University of Illinois
Manufactured in the United States of America

C 5 4 3 2 1

∞ This book is printed on acid-free paper.

Library of Congress Cataloging-in-Publication Data
Williams, William Carlos, 1883–1963.
Poems / William Carlos Williams ; introduction by
Virginia M. Wright-Peterson.
p.   cm.
Includes bibliographical references.
ISBN 0-252-02748-5 (cloth : alk. paper)
I. Title.
PS3545.I544P6   2002
811'.52—dc21   2001006450

POEMS

William Carlos Williams

INTRODUCTION

BY

VIRGINIA M. WRIGHT-PETERSON

UNIVERSITY OF ILLINOIS PRESS

URBANA AND CHICAGO

INTRODUCTION

INNOCENCE
REVISITED

Virginia M. Wright-Peterson

Innocence can never perish;
Blooms as fair in looks that cherish
Dim remembrance of the days
When life was young, as in the gaze
Of youth himself all rose-yclad,
Whom but to see is to be glad.
—William Carlos Williams, "Innocence"

SHORTLY AFTER FINISHING his medical internship in New York City in 1909, William Carlos Williams commissioned a printer in his hometown to publish his first book of poetry, entitled simply *Poems*.[1] Only a few of the poems have ever been republished because Williams asked his publisher, James Laughlin, not to include them in subsequent collections. James Laughlin and New Directions denied permission to republish until the work went out of copyright. By Williams's own admission in his autobiography, the "poems were bad Keats, nothing else—oh well, bad Whitman too. But I sure loved them. . . . There is not one thing of the slightest value in the whole thin booklet—except the intent."[2] It is almost impossible to recognize Williams as the author of the ornate, idealistic verse contained in *Poems,* since within four short years—by the time "The Wanderer" was published—he had begun writing with the stark language, vivid imagery, and unencumbered style for which he is ultimately known and celebrated. These earliest poems, while not masterpieces, are undeniably "connected parts of a living body of [his] work,"[3] and this "thin booklet" provides a window into the radical transformation of one of America's most esteemed voices during the advent of Modernism. Equally significant, the publication of *Poems* is part of the deeply personal story of an eminent writer's resilience and emergence at a time of disappointment and vulnerability, a saga of innocence lost and regained in the form of a vital new voice.

BEGINNINGS

Williams first became interested in writing during a convalescence in high school when he turned his attention from athletics to poetry.[4] A few years later, he met Ezra Pound at the University of Pennsylvania, where their student tenures overlapped in 1902 and 1903. The meeting was the beginning of a lifelong friendship and, to some extent, competition. Williams's medical program left little time for writing poetry; he had made the decision to earn his living in medicine rather endure the financial struggles that seemed inevitable for a poet.[5] In contrast, Pound dedicated himself to a writing vocation almost immediately and relocated to London in 1908 in that endeavor.

In that same year, 1908, life could not have been much better for Williams. At age twenty-five, he was nearing completion of his medical training, prospects looked good for an opportunity to join a practice on Park Avenue, he was in love with an enchanting woman at home, and he was writing poetry. However, within months—in the middle of the publishing of *Poems*—his charmed world shattered.

The first disappointment came when Williams's expectations for his medical practice dissolved. In the last months of his internship at Nursery and Child's Hospital in the Hell's Kitchen neighborhood of New York—after months of caring for some of the most destitute cases in the city under difficult circumstances—Williams refused to sign billing records without being permitted to verify them from the patient logs. In the process, he discovered a scheme of deception at the highest levels of the hospital administration, a situation that no one else in the medical community dared confront. Eventually, Williams quietly resigned and forfeited his hopes for a prestigious medical practice in New York.[6]

Instead, he returned home to Rutherford, to pursue alternative practice opportunities. While considering his options, Williams actively wrote poems and plays, he sang in a local production of *The Mikado*, and he was in the regular company of the woman he loved, Charlotte Herman, an aspiring concert vocalist and pianist, singing, playing duets, and reading his poetry to her. During these same months, Williams pulled together a collection of his poems and took them to Reid Howell, a local printer, for publication. It is likely that he was at least partially spurred to publish by Ezra Pound's recent success issuing *A Lume Spento* in the fall of 1908. The two men had continued to correspond regularly, sharing their writing aspirations.[7]

Williams sent a letter to his brother, Edgar, on March 18, 1909, describing his intentions for the book: "The book is at the press now I think or will be in a day or two. I think I shall keep about fifteen copies for myself and put all the rest on sale at thirty five cents at Garraway's old place. It scares me when I think of it. Only a hundred copies. Could you make me a sign to glue on card board: Poems by William C. Williams Limited Edition on sale now?"[8]

Poems, as originally published, had a taupe-chestnut–colored heavy-weight paper cover that simply read:

POEMS

By
WILLIAM C. WILLIAMS

RUTHERFORD
1909

The volume was small, about seven inches long and a little over four inches wide. Edgar, an award-winning architect who eventually designed many United States embassies and contributed to plans for the New York Public Library, designed the title page for *Poems*. The daisies, vines, and epigrams by Keats and Shakespeare invoke a nostalgia for the Romantic period and are reminiscent of the cover of an earlier edition of Whitman's *Leaves of Grass* and have the feel of the Art Nouveau movement, which was in full swing across the arts and architecture in the United States after originating in Europe.[9]

Despite the reserved enthusiasm that Williams expressed about his first publication, the poor reception it received resulted in a second significant disappointment. When the first edition arrived, his father made numerous corrections, mostly to the punctuation, apparently without much recognition of the content of the poems.[10] Williams sent the volume back to the printer with the corrections, and a revised edition was printed. His father's reaction to his work in this case, and probably in others, lingered with Williams for years. In notes made around 1950 in preparation for writing his autobiography, Williams recorded a dream he had shortly after his father died in 1918: "I'll never forget the dream. . . . I saw him coming down a peculiar flight of exposed steps, steps I have since identified as those before the dais of Pontius Pilate in some well-known painting. . . . I noticed him and with unspeakable joy cried out, 'Pop, so you're not dead!' But he only looked up at me over his right shoulder and commented severely, 'You know all that poetry you're writing. Well, it's *no good*.' I was left speechless and woke grumbling. I have never dreamed of him since."[11] Although this dream took place almost a decade after the publication of *Poems*, it poignantly illustrates the impact that his father's unfavorable opinion had.

His father was not his only critic. Williams sent Ezra Pound a copy of *Poems* and received back a letter dated May 21, 1909: "I hope to God you have no feelings. If you have, burn this before reading. . . . Individual, original it is not. . . . Your book would not attract even passing attention here [London]. . . . You are out of touch. That's all."[12] Pound recommended that Williams read Yeats, Browning, Francis Thompson, Swinburne, and Rossetti to learn about the recent progress of English poetry; he recommended Margaret Sackville, Rosamund Watson, Ernest Rhys, and Jim G. Fairfax as representative of what the "second rank can do." He suggested that Williams employ the first-person pronoun. The postscript is the only encouragement he offers: "And remember a man's real work is what *he is going to do,* not what is left behind him. Avanti e coraggio!"

In mid-June, Williams retrieved the inventory of books from Garraway's stationery store, where only four had sold. He gave a few to family members; the rest rotted and eventually burned in the printer's chicken coop where they were being stored.[13]

Throughout the loss of the medical practice opportunity and the discouraging reception that *Poems* received, Williams continued to court Charlotte Herman, describing her in a letter to his brother as "without a doubt the most delightful young lady I have met in a long time and I am inclined to recommend her to you rather perhaps too enthusiastically. . . . I went to see her one afternoon last week and we played duets for about three hours. . . . she is calm, intelligent, tactful, musical, . . . and [has a] most original bump of humor."[14] Perhaps Williams did recommend Charlotte too enthusiastically to Edgar. On

July 2, she and Edgar became engaged. Williams had an almost violent reaction to the news, and three days later, almost inexplicably, he proposed to Charlotte's younger sister, Florence. He admitted that he did not love her, but he was committed to come to love her.[15] His proposal could be seen as retaliatory or as an act of pale romanticism in contrast to the intense sexual drive that he confesses in his autobiography was a part of the "hidden core" of his life.[16]

By July of 1909, Williams's medical, artistic, and love prospects had dissolved. Edgar not only had the woman he loved but he had also won the Prix de Rome, a scholarship to study in Rome offered by the American Academy of Architects.[17] To partially compensate Williams for his losses and to allow him an opportunity to collect himself, his father funded a trip to Europe, ostensibly to complete a pediatrics fellowship.

A NEW WORLD NAKED

Williams left Rutherford in August, 1909, a few weeks after proposing to Florence Herman. He chose Leipzig as a destination, not so much for medical opportunities but because, as he notes in his autobiography, "I had been in love with the concert pianist [Charlotte Herman] who had spent three years there at the Conservatory."[18] Pound had encouraged him to come to London, but he resisted, perhaps still recovering from Pound's candid critique of *Poems,* or possibly because he intentionally wanted to distance himself from the English influence that many other expatriates like Pound and T. S. Eliot were adopting. Williams acknowledged that he was searching for a new form for his writing when he left: "a short form which would not be a sonnet."[19]

This solitary time in Europe, at a rather vulnerable juncture in his life, gave Williams an opportunity to glean inspiration from some Old World sources. Rather than continue to imitate them as he had in *Poems,* he began to use them as fodder in the creation of his new voice, one that would be reflective of the New World. Concentrated exposure to Richard Wagner, Martin Luther, and Heinrich Heine during the seven months Williams was in Germany contributed to the radical transformation of his writing.

Richard Wagner and "The Thing Itself"

Williams immersed himself in the arts while in Leipzig. He saw Ibsen's *Ein Puppenheim* and Schiller's *Die Räuber*, and heard Bach motets in addition to attending performances of Wagner's *Götterdämmerung* and Strauss's *Elektra*. In contrast, he found the medical work monotonous.[20]

Opera seemed especially to interest Williams. He had attended operas and various concerts in New York during his medical internships. He noted in his autobiography a particularly moving performance of Wagner's *Parsifal* that he had seen in 1906. Much later, in 1937, he spent a considerable amount of time working on a libretto, "The First President." In addition, Williams acknowledges Wagnerian influence on his first narrative poem. In his autobiography he notes that the setting for "Endymion," which preceded the 1909 volume of poems, was a Wagnerian forest.[21]

Williams's interest in opera, and in Wagner specifically, was not atypical in American culture in the early twentieth century; Wagner's works were performed extensively in the United States from 1870 to 1915 despite the extraordinary expense it took to stage them and the complicated copyright restrictions. In the United States, Wagner's operas were topics of intense debate and mixed reception. The complexity of the works could exasperate musicians and perplex audiences. Most often, though, sheer enthusiasm erupted, and the performances sent "magnetic shocks through audiences. One could hardly listen to *Götterdämmerung* among throngs of intense young enthusiasts without paroxysms of nervous excitement." One young music student declared that "a new world burst forth."[22] American enthusiasm for Wagner's art focused on his modernistic rebellion against Romantic ideals, his attempt to synthesize an entire work around one idea, and his juxtaposition of the sacred and the sensual.

While it may seem incongruous to suggest that Williams, who eventually attained a reputation for austerity in his poetry, was influenced by Wagner, whose works seem elaborate and opulent, Wagner's reputation as a cultural and artistic revolutionary would have appealed to Williams. Specifically, Wagner transformed operatic form from loosely constructed musical dramas to tightly focused works, as immense as they were, in which every aspect of the performance was constructed around one idea. He explained to Rossini that "everything contributes to the whole—nothing should remain secondary."[23] A critic writing at the turn of the century suggested that Wagner was a graphomaniac, who displayed a "stubborn perseverance in one and the same fundamental idea," which may account for Wagner's intense application of the leitmotiv.[24] Despite the dramatic and complex trappings of his operas, Wagner relentlessly pounds away at one idea, often redemption within the context of sensuality.

Williams saw *Götterdämmerung* in Germany in 1909. Its theme of redemption through unselfish, undying love forges the way for a new world and a new order. Williams might have felt this work was analogous to his commitment to Florence Herman, as he sought to achieve personal and artistic transformations through his dedication to that initially loveless engagement.

Martin Luther and Cultural Reform

Williams had long admired Martin Luther because of his rebellion against deeply embedded and powerfully protected traditions.[25] Williams made pilgrimages to two places of significance to Martin Luther while he was in Germany, and he based two poems on those visits. Shortly after arriving, he traveled to the convent ruins at Grimma outside of Leipzig. Katharina von Bora, who married Martin Luther, had been confined there against her will by church edict. When Luther and his followers aided the escape of eight nuns, including von Bora, on Easter Day 1523, they also agreed to support them by pragmatically marrying them. Their marriages were also acts of rebellion against church mandates on celibacy.[26]

There are similarities between von Bora's imprisonment and subsequent marriage to Luther and Williams's mother's life. After being orphaned, Elena Hoheb married William George Williams at fifteen, when financial and political circumstances in Puerto Rico prevented her brother from supporting her further.[27] Although he was not very sympathetic with his mother as a young man, Williams began to see that she, too, might have been bound in a marriage including less romantic love than she desired. He wrote to her after seeing Grimma and included a poem he dedicated to her.[28] The poem, "Ellen," the English form of his mother's name, opens with: "Thou priceless nun of a holy mind / . . . / Break from thy sleep in the darkness kind! / For me are the iron bars not strong" (1, 3–4). Not only was his mother's marriage potentially more pragmatic than romantic, when Williams made this trip he was contemplating a marriage to a person he hoped to come to love.

Luther's role as a liberator and reformer could have appealed to Williams when he was in the process of building a new life and a new form for his poetry. In March 1910, near the end of his stay in Leipzig, Williams made a pilgrimage to the small, stark quarters in Wartburg where Luther had lived before marrying von Bora. Williams identifies with Luther's prenuptial solitude in the poem he wrote about that visit, first entitled "Wartburg" and later "Martin and Katherine."

Alone today I mounted the steep hill
On which the Wartburg stands. Here Luther dwelt
In a small room a year through, here he spelt

. . . .

As now, it was March then. Lo! He'll fulfill
Today his weighty task! Sing for content. (1–3, 9–10)

The style of the poem, like that of "Ellen," is already strikingly different from the 1909 poems. Here Williams employs a more direct, first-person voice. He also explicitly draws parallels between his own life and Luther's: "As now, it was March then." The last lines express optimism that the task of reform ahead will be fulfilled: "Lo! He'll fulfill / Today his weighty task! Sing for content."

As in the case of his admiration of Wagner, Williams's interest in Luther was not unique among turn-of-the-century Americans; Luther was viewed as a vital cultural reformer in the United States. From 1880 to about 1910, the Vatican denounced Modernism as a particularly American movement. Resistance to papal criticism of Modernism went beyond religious and artistic potentates. President Theodore Roosevelt frequently referred to Luther as a fine example for Americans who were attempting to "shape the modern world."[29]

There is also an important connection between Wagner and Luther: Wagner's role as a cultural revolutionary can, in part, be attributed to his admiration of Luther. The German philosopher Nietzsche noted that perhaps Wagner's "finest, strongest, happiest, *most courageous* period" occurred when he was considering Luther's marriage. Nietzsche claimed that Wagner's work "Luther's Wedding" is a tribute to chastity *and* sensuality, and that Wagner should be lauded for demonstrating that there is no necessary antithesis between the two.[30] Although "Luther's Wedding" was never completed and was probably destroyed, Nietzsche's analysis of it documents Wagner's innovative approach to sensuality, which is potently evident in *Parsifal,* the opera that Williams saw in New York in 1906. This nondualistic treatment of sensuality as a path to redemption was one of the underlying causes of the significant public debate about the work in the United States and was probably quite relevant to William's thoughts on sensuality.

Heinrich Heine and Poetic Reform

Williams was also influenced by Heinrich Heine's poetry during his trip: "[Waking] early, I began to read to myself aloud, though softly, as I lay in bed, from Heine's *Buch der Lieder* [*Book of Songs*]. I had only recently got to know Heine well after finding a second-hand copy of his lyrics somewhere in a Leipzig bookstore just before quitting Germany. So there I lay intoning the poems one after another to myself. Beautiful things. I was learning several of them by heart."[31]

The poems published in *Buch der Lieder* were written from 1817 to 1827. At the time of Heine's death in 1856, *Buch der Lieder* was the most widely read book of poetry in the Western world.[32] The volume exudes expressions of unrequited love, rejects Romantic idealism, and employs an economical yet lyrical style, all of which were ultimately appealing to Williams.

The basis and extent of Heine's unrequited love is disputed; however, one possibility involves Heine's affection for his cousin Amalie, whom he courted in Hamburg in 1816. Letters he wrote that year indicate that he was distraught when she married someone else.[33] Further, Heine turned to Amalie's sister, in an act one biographer describes as a "pale attachment to the beloved's sister."[34] The biographical similarities to Williams's situation are striking. Heine's longing for his lost love permeates *Buch der Lieder;* all but a handful of the two hundred and forty poems focus on unrequited love, which would have been comforting to Williams after his recent loss of Charlotte Herman.

In addition to lamenting lost love, Heine was an important liberator and voice of social conscience. Matthew Arnold called him "a brave, yet a brilliant, a most effective soldier in the Liberation War of humanity."[35] Some of Heine's inspiration for invoking change originated in his admiration for Martin Luther. Heine wrote an essay celebrating Luther as "not only the greatest, but most thoroughly German hero of our history." He extolled Luther's role in freeing Germany from its own oppressions. Specifically, he notes Luther's role in "recognizing and legitimizing the most importunate claims of the senses . . . the priest becomes man, takes to himself a wife, and begets children, as God desires."[36]

Heine also recognizes Luther's ability as a translator and a poet. He notes Luther's role in translating the Bible from Latin into German, the everyday language of his people. Heine sought to use accessible language by writing with a common, nonidealized style that reflects the folk song and employs simple forms and metric lines of a conventional four-line stanza. He achieves poignancy through the tension he creates between simple, direct expressions and the complex ideas behind them. The following excerpt from "Lyrical Intermezzo" reflects many of these attributes:

A pine is standing lonely
In the North on a bare plateau.
He sleeps; a bright white blanket
Enshrouds him in ice and snow.
He's dreaming of a palm tree
Far away in the Eastern land
Lonely and silently mourning
On a sunburnt rocky strand.[37]

The minimal description of the tree in this poem reflects a surprisingly direct, unembellished style, given that it was written about 1822. The playful and ironic suggestion that the northern tree envies a palm tree without realizing that the palm is equally unhappy is characteristic of Heine.

While Heine's use of satire and irony was criticized by some of his contemporaries, few disputed the significance of his role in challenging the Romantic vision. "He liked to present himself as the last Romantic, at once Romanticism's harvester and gravedigger."[38] In one untitled poem in the preface of the 1839 of *Buch der Lieder,* Heine opens with a typically Romantic scene describing a nightingale singing under a fairy moon. The narrator subsequently comes across a deserted castle in an open glade guarded by a sphinx. Inspired by the nightingale's song, the narrator kisses the sphinx, causing it to come alive and drink the breath out of its prey, thereby suggesting that the world of the nightingale—emblematic of the sweetness and harmony in Romantic literature—is now dangerously deceptive; continuing to love and honor that tradition will be destructive, and perhaps fatal. Heine's intentional movement away from traditionally Romantic interpretations could have provided a model for Williams, who was seeking a new mode of expression after *Poems*.

Heine also found inspiration in Martin Luther's love of music: "his songs are particularly melodious . . . the *Marseillaise* of the Reformation, preserves to this day its inspiriting power."[39] Heine's poetry follows Luther's example by being imbued with musicality: "a great symphony made up of many and varied sounds."[40] One biographer claims that "no other poet excepting the Psalmist has been set to music as often as Heine."[41] More than five thousand musical interpretations have originated from the *Buch der Lieder* alone.[42] His writing has been set to music by Schubert (*Winterreise*), Schumann ("Die Grenadiere"), and Wagner, who became acquainted with Heine's poetry in 1830 when he was a student living in Leipzig. They met later on several occasions, and Wagner admitted to using Heine's poems as a basis for several librettos, including *Tannhäuser* and *Der Fliegende Holländer*. Wagner utilized passages of Heine's that emphasize lyrical innovation and themes of "individualism and a concrete view of life," themes that Williams adopted in his writing after 1909.[43]

HOMEWARD BOUND

After leaving Leipzig in March, Williams traveled for three more months throughout Europe before returning to Rutherford. He visited friends, including Ezra Pound, in England. He met his brother in Italy, and they traveled together for seven weeks through Venice, Florence, Rome, and Naples. Williams's last stop before sailing was the monastery at Santa Maria la Rabida, where Columbus had lived when he was discouraged that his projections of potential wealth overseas were being ignored. Williams was moved by the experience and noted in a letter to Florence Herman that the monastery, Columbus's home shortly before he claimed the new world, was the origin of the dream and promise of a break from tradition—a new world naked—the homeland he wanted to celebrate, rather than perpetuate homage to European ideals.[44] On May 23, 1910, he left Europe, returning to the Rutherford, New Jersey, where he ultimately established a life of medicine, marriage, and poetry with a new voice for the New World.

"NOTES FROM EUROPEAN TRIP, 1909–1910"

Evidence of the significance of the European trip can be found in a previously unpublished nine-page typescript entitled "Notes from European Trip, 1909–1910." The document is undated but it is likely that it was written between 1910 and 1913, and it incorporates material written before, during, and after the trip.[45] In addition, it shows a significant amount of editing in Williams's handwriting, probably done in 1916.[46] "Notes" is a loosely constructed narrative exhibiting little resemblance to *Poems*. It includes several oblique sketches of places Williams visited (Leipzig, Seville, Cordova, Antwerp, Wartburg, and Gibralter) and ten poems, or portions of poems, including "And Thus with All Praise," which was later published in *The Collected Poems of William Carlos Williams* along with the poem about Luther and von Bora, which originated in Leipzig.

The narrative is a collage that is part poem, part play, and part memoir. The tone is suddenly exclamatory and in first person, employing more colloquial language than Williams utilized in *Poems:* "Friends this world is somewhat a strange place / And will you hear me tell of it. . . . My mind is full of tall buildings with their tops hidden in mists." The woody dells and quiet brooks of *Poems* have been replaced with "cities with smoke" and "a filthy tree." Williams is searching for and finding truth and beauty locally, more and more in the accessible present and the everyday. One line claims that "There can be no great art until simple terms have been given a meaning by universal personal heroism and disregard of self."

"Modern Invocation," one of the longest poems included within "Notes," explicitly signals the birth of a new voice and liberation from lamenting lost or distant beauty and truth:

Rise in the air with a roar of wings spirits,

. . . .

. . . Then let the old be met
Midway in air . . .

. . . .

And sing of the modern young man
Journeying to freedom, sing!

The poem expresses the "hell of modern desire / That cannot go on ships as Odyssus the Greek hero did / . . . / . . . Sing of the new / Sing of the here! . . . / Also sing with beauty not always sweet! / Sing of pain and the terror of ignorance!" In "Modern Invocation" Williams abandons visions of truth and beauty based on idealistic images and elaborate wording.

"Modern Invocation" and another untitled poem embedded in "Notes" that was subsequently published as "And Thus with All Praise" vividly anticipate "The Wanderer" (1914), a work that most critics identify as the turning point in Williams's career—the debut of his unique voice, a voice independent of past icons and European dominance. It is also the poem Williams noted was the basis for his magnum opus "Paterson."[47] There are many similarities between "And Thus with All Praise" and "The Wanderer." "And Thus with All Praise" begins with a line exulting women: "Wonderful creatures! / Why must I call you Bride and Mother? / . . . / Be to me deeds of compassion; / Have these for name, none other." A "horse-godmother" appears in "Notes," resembling the grandmother who is the vital muse in "The Wanderer." "Modern Invocation" refers to listening in his own land, hearing and interpreting to his people, which sounds reminiscent of "How shall I be a mirror to this modernity" in "The Wanderer."

Another poem in "Notes," "In Socialasia," celebrates laborers: "God bless the merry working man / . . . // How shall I keep him ignorant?" These lines empathize with the workers who are being replaced by machines. Williams remained committed to working-class causes throughout his career; a mill strike in 1913 appears in "The Wanderer" and "Paterson." Although Williams never published "Notes from European Trip, 1909–1910" in its entirety, it is an experimentation with the voice that later appears in "The Wanderer" and ultimately "Paterson," giving every indication that it is a source he mined for decades.

FROM *POEMS* TO "THE WANDERER" AND BEYOND

The transformation in Williams's writing from 1909 to the time of writing "The Wanderer" in 1913 is the result of a wide variety of experiences, most of which have already been extensively explored and documented: the Armory Show in 1913—including associations with Charles Demuth and Alfred Stieglitz—the Paterson silk-worker strike in 1913, the rise of Imagism, and Williams's rereading of Whitman's poetry with renewed vigor. Our consideration of *Poems* and of his subsequent European trip add another thread to understanding how and why Williams became the poet he did.

Despite the ornate, nineteenth-century language and imagery that permeate *Poems,* the volume also contains glimpses of the later Williams. Traces of his shift to colloquial language and his increasing emphasis on the local and present are evident in a few of the poems. "A Street Market, N.Y., 1908" presents a striking contrast to the idealistic scenes of nature that dominate most of the collection. Descriptions such as "the drab sheet is drawn," "[i]n the grey street," and "[s]eething below / Now with eccentric throe / The thick souls ebb and flow" in

"A Street Market" are juxtaposed with the woody dells, quiet brooks, and woodland breezes found in the other poems. "A Street Market" opens with the narrator's confession that he had been "Blind to a patent wide reality, / But this new day / Has brought a rich array" and that he is now able to recognize its significance—"There History / Welds her gold threads in glittering brilliant show." This is one of the first times that Williams celebrates an everyday scene and finds beauty in the quotidian. "A Street Market, N.Y., 1908" ends by admiring the masses of Kaffirs, Jews, Slavs, Teutons, and Greeks haggling over "bread and brew" and then singing "sweet songs forever new."

James E. B. Breslin notes in *William Carlos Williams: An American Artist* that throughout most of the *Poems,* Williams employs a Platonic approach to the ideal, in which the poet sees himself as an alienated outsider, while poetic and female beauty is remote and distant.[48] This traditional perspective of alienation from the ideal is evident throughout the volume, especially in "The Loneliness of Life" where the poet seems to lament, "Could I but breast this overwhelming tide / This torrent of mortality . . . // [and] cast upon the prospect wide / My heedful stare; map out with eager hand / All realms around . . . / I'd choose me one," though his actual state is one of rootlessness and even ignorance—"These fields I know not; know not whence I come." The female personification of the ideal, as well as the poet's sense of alienation, is presented in several of the poems, although perhaps most prominently in "To Simplicity," opening with the assertion, "Thou first born nymph of any woody dell, / Thee have I lost, O sweet Simplicity," which later becomes a heartfelt plea: "Where art thou hid? Cry, cry again! I come! I come! I come!"

In addition to the fact that many of the poets, including Keats, whom Williams had been imitating reflected a Platonic position, Williams may have also been reflecting the remoteness of his relationship with his parents, which greatly influenced his early publications. Critics note that Williams was torn between his sensual yearnings and a desire to remain obedient to his parents, whom most biographers agree were emotionally distant, aristocratic, and Victorian.[49] Breslin asserts that Williams needed to rebel against the "high aspirations, strict morality, and personal aloofness" of his parents, or he would have been destined to write "polite, nostalgic verses" for the *New Yorker* and he would have become a "neat, orderly, prosperous physician who would 'never think anything / but a white thought.'"[50]

There is ample evidence in *Poems* of the tension Williams felt between his passionate, sensual self and the aristocratic presence his parents endorsed. In "The Uses of Poetry," a poem originally dedicated to Hilda Doolittle (H.D.),[51] he and a lady intend, after they "close the door of sense," to escape on "posey's transforming giant wing" to "worlds afar whose fruits all anguish mend." The conflict he feels between the parts of his divided self in the context of pressure he felt from his father and competition with his brother is also evident in "To My Better Self." The narrator in this poem seeks, perhaps ironically, "everlasting peace" in a post-Edenic world. The poem captures, again probably ironically, tension between father, Adam, and brothers, Cain and Abel, in the sonnet form usually reserved for expressions of romantic love.

Further evidence that Williams was attempting to reconcile a private self and a proper, public self is that he maintained notebooks of unpublished works that contrast with the form and content of what he was initially willing to disclose in a public forum. In his autobiography, Williams gives an account of notebooks he kept where he "reserved [his] Whitmanesque 'thoughts,' a sort of purgation and confessional, to clear my head and my heart from turgid obsessions" in contrast to the Keatsian style that he "copied religiously." Maintenance of two sets of books accounts for the fact that after the trip to Leipzig, Williams wrote "Notes from European Trip, 1909–1910" in a new experimental form, and yet he reverted to classical language and form in *Tempers*, which was published in 1913. He was not ready to publish his experimental voice and liberate himself publicly from his parents. *Tempers*, which is dedicated to his Uncle Carlos and includes several translations that express homage to his Spanish heritage, appears to be a tribute to his family and his European roots rather than a work representing his eventual aesthetics, striving to establish a uniquely American voice.

Although, as noted, *Poems* reflects primarily the public, Keatsian, proper self, both "A Street Market, N.Y., 1908" and "On Thinking of a Distant Friend" reveal that Williams was beginning to recognize the ideal and the sublime in the everyday and present—a local experience rather than one distant in time and place. "On Thinking of a Distant Friend" opens by recording a tired narrator, probably close kin to Williams at the end of a long day at the hospital: "Up stairs and stairs I climb, the final task / Of all the day's continual duties done." Although the poem is still expressed in a tightly controlled form and ornate language—"cumbrous mists," "feathery sleep," "princely boon"—it records the transcendental possibilities of an everyday moment filled with the pleasure and enchanting powers of the simple memory of a lady friend: "O fullest moon! Thou who on her dost gaze and yet on me // Far distant; thou hast filled my lazy mind / With gentlest ponderings! Enchantress kind, / To at a breath breathe round such ecstasy!" William begins to demonstrate that the ideal is accessible in common daily events and that the poet needs not be alienated from it—a significant attribute of his later work, evident in "The Wanderer" when the narrator finds transcendence in baptism in the filthy water of a local river and beauty in the old hag grandmother who is the muse.

Although it took a few years for Williams to abandon strict rhyme schemes and traditional poetic patterns, and to simplify his language, *Poems* reveals that he had already begun to focus on reconciling sensuality and redemption and to realize that the ideal can be found in everyday experiences. The European trip—especially the seven months he spent in Leipzig exposed to the works of Wagner, Luther, and Heine—helped liberate him from the artistic and cultural traditions he had previously imitated. At a vulnerable point in his personal and professional life, Williams assimilated aspects of Old World Europe and utilized three of its cultural icons to help release him so that he could follow the instincts that were hinted at earlier in the "thin booklet" he self-published and later shunned.

INNOCENCE REGAINED

Williams's publisher and scholars have resisted defying his request that *Poems* not be republished, a request that was initially made very early in his career, long before his place in American letters was secure. Now, when there is no question that his position in the canon is safe, it seems appropriate to study *Poems* for a better understanding of the origins of Williams's writing, especially the cataclysmic transformation that took place at the precise time that Virginia Woolf claimed that "human character changed . . . all human relations [had] shifted . . . including religion, conduct, politics, and literature," a change she claims occurred "on or about December, 1910," exactly when Williams was in Germany.[52] Some, like T. S. Eliot and Ezra Pound, continued on the high road of Modernism, creating works that incorporate extensive allusions to the masters of the past. Others, like Williams, struck out and found meaning in the streets of their hometowns, in their backyards, and in unlikely places such as on the road to the hospital for the contagious.

Although, in retrospect, Williams was not proud of these first poems, he noted in an interview with the *New York Herald Tribune* in 1932 that each of his poems is "in tune with the tempo of [my] life—scattered, yet welded into a whole, broken, yet woven together."[53] One critic adds that in "the welding and the weaving one discovers the techniques (often brilliant) of Williams' poetry."[54]

NOTES

1. William Carlos Williams, *Poems* (Rutherford, N.J.: Williams, 1909).

2. William Carlos Williams, *The Autobiography of William Carlos Williams* (New York: New Directions, 1951), 107.

3. Rod Townley, *The Early Poetry of William Carlos Williams* (Ithaca: Cornell University Press, 1975), 16.

4. Williams, *Autobiography*, 46–47.

5. Williams, *Autobiography*, 49–52.

6. Paul Mariani, *William Carlos Williams: A New World Naked* (New York: McGraw-Hill, 1981), 74.

7. Mariani, *Williams*, 76.

8. Williams, to Edgar Williams, 18 Mar. 1909, Beinecke Rare Book and Manuscript Collection at Yale University.

9. Townley, *Early Poetry*, 40.

10. A copy of the edited volume resides in the Beinecke Rare Book and Manuscript Collection at Yale University.

11. William Carlos Williams, "Some Notes Towards an Autobiography," unpublished, Beinecke Rare Book and Manuscript Collection at Yale University.

12. Ezra Pound to Williams, 21 May 1909, in *William Carlos Williams: The Critical Heritage*, ed. Charles Doyle (Boston: Routledge, 1980), 50–51.

13. Williams, *Autobiography*, 108.

14. Williams, to Edgar Williams, 18 Mar. 1909.

15. Mariani, *Williams*, 78–79.

16. Williams, *Autobiography*, xii.

17. Williams, *Autobiography*, 108–9.

18. Williams, *Autobiography*, 109.

19. Williams, *Autobiography*, 110.

20. Williams, *Autobiography*, 110.

21. Williams, *Autobiography*, 59.

22. John Dizikes, *Opera in America: A Cultural History* (New Haven: Yale University Press, 1993), 243.

23. Edmond Michotte, *Richard Wagner's Visit to Rossini (Paris 1860); and, An Evening at Rossini's in Beau Sejour (Passy) 1858*, trans. Herbert Weinstock (Chicago: University of Chicago Press, [1968]), 66–67.

24. Alex Ross, "Wagner's Legacy of Beauty and Hatred," *New Yorker*, 10 Aug. 1998, 66.

25. Mariani, *Williams*, 88.

26. Henry Eyster Jacobs, *Martin Luther: The Hero of the Reformation, 1483–1546* (New York: Putnam's, 1898), 264.

27. Mariani, *Williams*, 16.

28. Mariani, *Williams*, 84.

29. Harmut Lehmann, *Martin Luther in the American Imagination*, American Studies: A Monograph Series, vol. 63 (Munich: Wilhelm Fink Verlag, 1988), 252.

30. Friedrich Wilhelm Nietzsche, *On the Genealogy of Morals* (1887), trans. and ed. Walter Kaufmann in *The Basic Writings of Nietzsche* (New York: Modern Library, [1968]), 534.

31. Williams, *Autobiography*, 118.

32. Hanna Spencer, *Heinrich Heine*, ed. Ulrich Weisstein (Boston: Twayne, 1982), 12.

33. Jeffery L. Sammons, *Heinrich Heine: A Modern Biography* (Princeton: Princeton University Press, 1979), 43.

34. Max Brod, *Heinrich Heine: The Artist in Revolt*, trans. Joseph Witriol (London: Valentine & Mitchell, 1956), 156.

35. Matthew Arnold, *Essays in Criticism: First Series* (New York: Macmillan, 1924), 192–93 and 158.

36. Heinrich Heine, "Religion and Philosophy in Germany," in *Heine's Prose and Poetry* (New York: Dutton, 1966), 256–57.

37. Heinrich Heine, *The Complete Poems of Heinrich Heine: A Modern Version*, trans. Hal Draper (Boston: Suhrkamp/Insel, 1982), sec. 33.

38. Sammons, *Heine*, 59.

39. Heine, "Religion," 259.

40. Brod, *Heine*, 154.

41. Sammons, *Heine*, 65.

42. Spencer, *Heine*, 16.

43. Brod, *Heine,* 200.

44. Mariani, *Williams,* 88.

45. Williams wrote the poem on p. 5 of "Notes" that begins "Hark Hilda" in 1906 as a birthday greeting for Hilda Doolittle (H.D.). Note that the initial letters of each line spell "Hilda" (Mariani, *Williams,* 45).

46. A. Walton Litz and Christopher MacGowen, *The Collected Poems of William Carlos Williams,* vol. 1 (New York: New Directions, 1991.), 475. A note in this volume dates a poem that also appears in "Notes from European Trip, 1909–1910" as having been written between 1910 and 1912.

47. Williams, *Autobiography,* 60–61.

48. James E. B. Breslin, *William Carlos Williams: An American Artist* (New York: Oxford University Press, 1970), 11.

49. Townley, *Early Poetry,* 35.

50. Breslin, *Williams,* 7.

51. Breslin, *Williams,* 11.

52. Virginia Woolf, "Mr. Bennett and Mrs. Brown," *New York Evening Post,* 17 Nov. 1923.

53. Williams, interview, *New York Herald Tribune,* 18 Jan. 1932.

54. Townley, *Early Poetry,* 17.

POEMS

BY

W.C. WILLIAMS.

~Happy Melodist~ for~
ever piping Songs for~
ever new. ~Keats.~
~So all my best is press~
ing Old Words new ~
~Spending again what~
is already spent. ~.~
~Shakespeare~

1909

INNOCENCE

Innocence can never perish;
Blooms as fair in looks that cherish
Dim remembrance of the days
When life was young, as in the gaze
Of youth himself all rose-yclad,
Whom but to see is to be glad.
For wherein lies the chasm wide
Which seer and schoolboy should divide?
'Tis but the sum of paltry years,
Filled, what if, with laugh and tears?
These are offspring of the earth.
Innocence hath heavenly birth!
Smiles were naught e'er life begun,
And what are tears when life is done?
These experience teach but wonder
Rides through all, above and under.
Like to gaudy winged flies,
With cap in hand and fixed eyes,
Which children chase but capture n'er
And innocence and wonder share
Sweet sisterhood with mystery.
Oh, blessed and triumphant three!

Then cry once more ye sages blest!
Once more give voice! Attest! Attest!
That wonders still with age increase,
Nor e'er grow less, nor ever cease;
And innocence is wonder's kin.
Who'll raise the latch and let her in?

TO SIMPLICITY

Thou first born nymph of any woody dell,
Thee have I lost, O sweet Simplicity,
All in the crooked shade and cannot tell
Where thou art hidden; but when lacking thee
I care no more to live; how sad, then, sad a youth am I.

Thee have I sought by every grove and rill
Which once I loved, that oft were frequented
By thy blest feet, but though I wandered still
At noonday, vanished went thou ever, fled
To farther nooks. Would chanting birds me thither too had led!

Oh I could weep! had not mine eyes forbad
Days gone the folly.—I would on, but where?
Ah me, I'll sigh no more, no more be sad
But here sit down and sing thy praises, fair,
As true as heart can prompt and voice mount music's even stair.

Thee once I saw beside a quiet brook
Where lately thou hadst bathed and troth, thine eyes
Were clearer than the stream; thy hair which shook
Unto the grass was as the leaf which tries
To kiss the water's brim, no more, when gradual currents rise.

Thine arms were as the little pebbles white
And round as they but packed a thousandfold
More full with grace; thy lips were berries light
Red berries on an autumn tree. All told
How rare thy beauty is.—Oh, that thee might I now behold!

And once I saw thee tiptoe and o'erpeep
A hedge of green where sure a linnet sang
Most happily, which but to hear, asleep

Fell soon thy breath. Hark! Hark! Mine ears are numb
With dread! Methought a faint hallooing rang!
Where art thou hid? Cry, cry again! I come! I come! I come!

JUNE

Youthful June tricked out in loose attire,
Thee all along thy flowery scented way
I follow, singing o'er that love-worn lay
Thy traitorous birds have taught me. Sweet, aspire

No more the distant balmy-blossomed briar
To find, urge not thy doting feet, but stay.
But stay dear pensive wanderer and allay
These pangs thy lover owns for thy desire.

Now art thou couched in such a breathless dell
As those same feathery songsters seek, when rise
Unto their hearts such throes as bid them flee

All peopled haunts; such throbs as in me dwell;
For, oh, I love thee, and in such fond wise,
I cannot brook denial! Live aye with me!

BALLAD OF TIME
AND THE PEASANT

Old Time was sitting in the sun.
  Sing hey for father Time!
And for he felt so full of fun
  He warbled in gay rhyme.

"Come nigh me shepherd worn and sad,
  What is thy passion? Speak!
N'er have I seen so grave a lad
  This livelong April week."

And then I told him, Margaret,
  Of all thy cruelty,
Until at last his cheeks were wet
  With whimpering for me.

I told him thou wouldst kiss me, Sweet,
  But ten times in an hour
And often wouldst thou fail to meet
  But merely for a shower.

That ever wilt thou waste away
  Nigh half the pleasant night,
In heavy sleep, and never stay
  Until the morrow bright.

That scarce we're met when thou art fled
  Adistant from my side
To waste thy lips on milk and bread.
  Oh, heartless cruel bride!

And Time made answer: "Nay, good youth";
    Sing hey for father Time!
"In twenty years I'll tell thee truth,
    Such merit hath thy ryhme."

TO HIS LADY
WITH A QUEER NAME

Love, change thy name! Elizabeth
Is apter far. For then a breath
Could smoothly ride it, when 'twere meet
To lisp in praise of thee my sweet.

For what's a name that doth express
No inkling of a daintiness;
A soft demeanor when 'tis there
But veil to make the fair less fair?

But nay, reveil thee and repine
Against thy love so asinine!
For fairer wert than now thou art,
How soon wouldst find some other's heart.

THE USES OF POETRY

I've fond anticipation of a day
O'erfilled with pure diversion presently,
For I must read a lady poesy
The while we glide by many a leafy bay,

Hid deep in rushes, where at random play
The glossy black winged May-flies, or whence flee
Hush-throated nestlings in alarm,
Whom we have idly frighted with our boat's long sway.

For, lest o'ersaddened by such woes as spring
To rural peace from our meek onward trend,
What else more fit? We'll draw the light latch-string

And close the door of sense; then satiate wend,
On poesy's transforming giant wing,
To worlds afar whose fruits all anguish mend.

THE QUEST OF HAPPINESS

This much, I find, must then be also true,
If naught of worldly goods to own be best:
'Tis nothing worth to waste, in fiery quest
Of proper lands disposal, pleasure's due

Proportioned minute; that which is to do,
That will be done, through laws not manifest
At this young season; but shall each possessed
Fine soul some sweet perfection deeply brew.

True having lives but only in the mind;
And there dwells pleasure, all delightful things
Find there soft resting nooks to revel in,

And there is nothing corporal confined.
Then loose ye all, ye earthly bonds which cling
About my heart, and—life's new song, begin!

JULY

Hot cheeked July, with lusty sinews primed
For deeds of passion, hail! and halt afar!
Thou wild incontinent, thy fiery star
Hath sanctioned in thee dreams to naught atimed

But thine own reckless humors. All o'ergrimed
With dust and sweat art thou, which, jointly, mar
Thine else smooth, well-watched bulk, till many a scar
Quick fancy sees there aptly pantomimed.

Thee near about thy dense dominions roll;
Choked, weighted down with greens in mad excess;
With cumbrous trees; and intertangling vines;

Which round among walks none in hempen stole
But storms instead a wild and wayward press
Where Action's brazen helmet solely shines.

IMITATIONS

I.

O flee from me, find me not, call me not love!
Complain not I slight thee, withhold thy vain tear;
For I can but wrong thee, thou never canst move
This bondless, wild heart to inhabit thy sphere.

True, thee do I cherish, but not to be bound;
My passion rides over and on past thy ken;
Then fly! O abandon me, ere thou has found
What wreck can such anguish inflict upon men.

II.

I saw three children frollicking,
    Three naked little boys,
In shallow brook with shout and spring
    And wild delightful noise;
I saw the age-wrung, giant trees
Loom darkly o'er with peaceful swing
    Upon the summer breeze.

Hand clasped in hand they sprang around,
    Nor dared to plunge alone
But sang a ballad then with bound
    All three dipped in as one.
The singing ceased, the bubbles flew,
As panting leaped they from the ground
    With cheeks of crimson hue.

Thus, o'er and o'er with joy unchecked
    They sprang and dipped and rose;
The pool around with foam was flecked;
    They dreamt not of repose.
The river night ran swift along
And bore me on and nothing wrecked
    How swiftly waned the song.

The singing ceased, far, far behind
    The giant trees grew small,
But still I carry in my mind
    That merry madrigal,
And still I see the age-wrung trees
And hear the tinkling water, fall
    And feel the woodland breeze.

LOVE

Love is twain, it is not single,
Gold and silver mixed to one,
Passion 'tis and pain which mingle
Glist'ring then for aye undone.

Pain it is not; wondering pity
Dies or e'er the pang is fled:
Passion 'tis not, foul and gritty,
Born one instant, instant dead.

Love is twain, it is not single,
Gold and silver mixed in one,
Passion 'tis and pain which mingle
Glist'ring then for aye undone.

TO A FRIEND

Sweet Lady, sure it seems a thousand years
Since last you honored me with gentle speech.
Yet, when, forsaking fantasy, I reach
With memory's index o'er the stretching tiers

Of minutes wasted, counting, (as who fears
Strict-chiding reason, lest it should impeach
All utterance, must) a mighty, gaping breach
'Twixt truth and seeming verity appears.

What means it then but that each hour, a snail,
With thee adistant, has crept halting by?
They have been ages, leaving me an old

Methuselah in thought's account, yet hale
In truth's and young and poor as e'er, or nigh.
To pray you greet me then, say is't o'er bold?

TO MY BETTER SELF

Good, honest part of me, I bid thee pray
Bestir thyself, for by lost Eden, I,
Thy father Adam, can naught other say
Than that thy brother Cain surpasses thee

In manly thrift. I know thee patient, true;
But yet there is a time when patience checks
Ambition's worthy course. Thou needs must view
Our favor with some ardor; sure it wrecks

Thee something if we smile? Then here should lie
Thy purposed but: to live in our commend.
And for the rest, look to thy brother, he
Is ample scripture for a text. Amend

At once thy ways that all discord may cease
And age stretch out to everlasting peace.

A STREET MARKET, N.Y., 1908

Eyes that can see,
Oh, what a rarity!
For many a year gone by
I've looked and nothing seen
    But ever been
Blind to a patent wide reality.

    But this new day
    Has brought a rich array.
Like merchant silks in tray
When the drab sheet is drawn
    And breaks a dawn
Streaked, fretted, flecked, with hues of flowery May.

    In the grey street
    Now my spread eyelids greet
Amassed, evolving, fleet,
Glimpses of mighty change;
    Endless in range;
Stretching from ice and ice to tropic heat.

    Seething below
    Now with eccentric throe
The thick souls ebb and flow.
Far tribes there mingle free,
    There History
Welds her gold threads in glittering brilliant show.

    Kaffir and Jew
    Commerce for bread and brew;

There die the wars which grew
When first was quarrelling
    And gaily sing
Slavs, Teutons, Greeks, sweet songs forever new.

    Eyes that can see,
    Oh, what a rarity!
For many a year gone by
I've looked and nothing seen
    But ever been
Blind to a patent wide reality.

SEPTEMBER

Rich September, season bountiful,
Maturity, with ripe fruit plenished horn.
Stalks midmost in thy pageant; earliest morn,
With instep glistening dew, the timeful lull

And following fall of scythe doth hear; thy dull
Night paths full-frocked Lucina doth adorn
That laden carts may thread them; and the worn,
Sleep hampered farmer wakes, his corn to hull.

And thus all leases in thee come to term;
And spring's desire attains accomplishment;
And worldly thrift finds nothing left undone;

And labor rests, and talks with those infirm
Beside the fire who stay and wonderment
Starts up to hear their prophecies begun.

THE LONELINESS OF LIFE

Could I but breast this overwhelming tide,
This torrent of mortality, and stand
Glittering in sunlight on the green, high land
Whose slopes first tamed then bade that torrent glide;

Then would I cast upon the prospect wide
My heedful stare; map out with eager hand
All realms around from whence at last, well scanned,
I'd choose me one, and there would I abide.

But now among low plains or banks which rear
Their flower hung screens o'erhead I wander—where?
These fields I know not; know not whence I come;

Nor aught of all which spreads so touching near.
The very bird-songs I have heard them n'er
And this strange folk they know not e'en my name.

WISTFULNESS IN IDLENESS

Oh, for a song!
A song and a sorrow!
And time to regret;
Aye and time to forget.
Oh, the balm of tomorrow!
The boon of a song!

ON THINKING OF A DISTANT FRIEND

Up stairs and stairs I climb, the final task
Of all the day's continual duties done;
Nor dream of aught more sweet, now hath the sun
In cumbrous mists descended, than to bask

In his fast fading light awhile, then ask
Of night a heavy draught and straight begun
With lying down in feathery sleep, o'errun
A hundred ebon courses. But O mask!

O mask unkept of heaven! what princely boon
Hast thou held dark till now? O fullest moon!
Thou who on her dost gaze and yet on me

Far distant; thou hast filled my lazy mind
With gentlest ponderings! Enchantress kind,
To at a breath breathe round such ecstasy!

TO A LADY

Sunshine is to spring so constant
None but slights that warm regard,
But with winter's winds remonstrant
Then sense stands, all doors unbarred.

Thus we find there's naught but wearies,
Oft repeated all things tire,
While an unexpected tear is
Sometimes food for pleasure's fire.

Then farewell, though I adore thee,
Bid me haste to leave thy side,
Lest to have me e'er before thee
Thy love too be sorely tried.

TO THE UNKNOWN LADY

So shall thy praise, thou whom I love so well
As praise long spent grow stale and meaningless,
Yielding to Time, who still doth bid men spell
More deep and deep to Wonder's wilderness.

For, not thine arm which wields a huntress' spear,
Nor shall thy lovely parts, nor shall thy grace,
These outworn badges of some vanished peer,
Awake that fire which bids all these give place.

But 'tis thy mind, that realm of sovereignty,
That viewless orb, that world in duplicate,
That more than world, from whose empowered see
Quick doubling fancy holds unrivaled state.

Yet when this praise too, wears, my love shall hold,
In iron crowns rusted as gleams the untouched gold.

NOVEMBER

Hail, thou month of final fruits and snow!
All hail, November, who dost see the end
Of harvest and bleak winter's birthday! Rend
With tempest the gigantic air! aye blow

The grievous trumps! for doth thy season know
Most cause for bitterness! Thou hast seen bend
All greens unto decay; a dying trend
In everything; wail then to sate thy woe!

And, if thy time is sorrows, let all breath
Breathe dirgeful music for is welcome such,
Nor shall the stricken curse that thou dost hold

Ingratitude a minion. Rail at death,
Thou sufferer! for anon at his fell touch
Thou too shalt wither and grow sudden cold.

ON A PROPOSED TRIP SOUTH

They tell me on the morrow I must leave
This winter eyrie for a southern flight
And truth to tell I tremble with delight
At thought of such unheralded reprieve.

E'er have I known December in a weave
Of blanched crystal, when, thrice one short night
Packed full with magic, and O blissful sight!
N'er May so warmly doth for April grieve.

To in a breath's space wish the winter through
And lo, to see it fading! Where, oh, where
Is caract could endow this princely boon!

Yet I have found it and shall shortly view
The lush high grasses, shortly see in air
Gay birds and hear the bees make heavy droon.

THE FOLLY OF PREOCCUPATION

There enters no thing scatheless from the womb;
But imperfection clings all forms about.
Nor leaf, nor flower, nor pod, nor seeding plume,
But some regard shall find, than this, less stout;

And beasts there be with cloven nostrils born,
And birds that tear their young, and eyeless things;
But man more curst, more twisted, ruthless torn,
For each of these a shriveled thousand brings.

Yet to man's eyes, He who, all these can see,
Constrained to throb in just apportioned space,
Should all-pervading all perfection be.

What else than this can wisdom then out-face?
That all these shows like strains of song shall flee
Which man to try out solely here hold place.

THE BEWILDERMENT OF YOUTH

Man perplexed by detail in his youth
O'erstares his world; views forms which myriad seem,
Distracting here, there, each with changing gleam,
Like fireflies pointing midnight's curtain smooth.

And all his purpose stands amazed, unknit
By wonder, knowing naught of where nor why,
Compassed about with fresh variety
Where'er his chancing eager looks may flit.

But with his age at length he fade this out:
That these but aspects are of scant things true;
And as he ages more, more few and few
Becomes this late engrossing, formless rout;

Until he sees, when life is almost done,
These final few go mingling into one.

THE BEWILDERMENT OF AGE

How can I else than ponder on these things;
How weakest back must bear the hugest load;
And wills unpropped feel most temptation's stings;
And helpless slaves most cringe neath iron goad.

These things do stick unsolved upon my view;
Or this the end; that strength alone can live,
And mercy doth no heavenly heart imbue,
And law no trespass ever hence forgive.

Unthinkable if life rank more than death.
Then, for there is none other sounder way,
I can naught answer and still crave a breath,
But: "As the soundless infinite blue day

This mystery outbounds my little ken;"
Then be content it rests with more than men.

HYMN TO THE SPIRIT OF FRATERNAL LOVE

Thou heaven-sprung flame which for man's good most needs must
    flare,
Dear brother love, as those fond shepherds round the tide
Of Galilee, cast scattering o'er the stone strewn, bare,
And fruitless earth their fragrant pyres, then flung awide
Depths uncontrolled of heart, for thee to dwell in and illume,
    Thus, thus, would I!

And lo! the damasked hordes of flattery all take wing!
But leave me rather bare, with crooked arms outspread
Into the breath of winter, writhing neath her sting;
Than cloaked in hectic splendor, like those regal dead,
Of Egypt who, in ghastly festal trim, one further vain day through
    Must smile unfed.

Then hail! sweet spirit, threading night's un'customed maze
With gracious toll (though wild tempestuous is that night.)
And for thine own this lone luxuriant heart appraise;
And, if 'tis worthy, roam no more but here find might
And tillage broad and seasons fair which love thy fruitful sway
    And grant thee gain.

HYMN TO PERFECTION

For thee, O Perfection, great ruler,
Chief God of all monarchs, I shatter
The stillness of heaven; awaken,
Like waves on an ocean which scatter
A widening tempest, the uproar.

And cry who will, "Pile the bare mountains,
All rock, in gigantic confusion!
Aye, let every desperate bellow
Of sea, earth and sky in collusion
From tripling trumpet be blasted
Upon the huge pillar! Profusion
Of space so engirds thee, as ever,
Thou wouldst hold undisrupted seclusion."

But not I! One with man, yet immortal;
For me hast thou built no constriction.
This heart doth outvie the weak eagle.
Not sight so o'errides all restriction.
Then hail! thou great God, from my woodlands
I sing, and Thou calm'st my affliction!

NOTES FROM EUROPEAN TRIP,
1909–1910

A man must be unhealthy for progress. Disintegration must set in before there can be readjustment.

God be lauded that I posess you
Ah God that I shall never see you again!

Patience is a filthy tree with roots in the air and branches and reaves underground.

Love is a pied mosaic.

See the birdies there! See them! Taking their breakfast. They stuff themselves! (Deep breath.) They always breathe the fresh air - so fresh all the time. But some die in the winter - dont you thing so? They freeze.

You , yourself are too hard. Always remember that teacher - that S Spaniard - he was a painter. (Taking up a plate.) You would bring him a drawing:
(Mimics with the plate.) Bien, muy bien! Um, a little out of proportion here: and here too dark -" and he would finish by saying the whole thing was wrong. But it was always: " Bien, muy bien!" just the same.

Cardinal de Retz:
        " Well you see he was still young, he still had many true thoughts. Afterward they get mixed up in politics."

Mr. P. has three remedies and he'll live just as long as any one else: salt, kerosene and cod liver oil.

Art is the maturity of the adventure of love.

The purgative effect of tragedy lies in the boinging down of all that is high and the raising up of all that is low to one common ground of helplesness. It is always enobling to him who has the forces of truth in his heart and sees the miserliness of men, impudent and safe.

Theoe can be no great art until simple terms have been given a meaning
by universal personal heroism and disregard of self, a physical heroism.

The secret of life is to do useless things with the utmost vigor.

One realizes the buisness of afternoon functions when he sees a num-
ber of twenty year females turning into an entry and reflects that it is
his engagement to one of them that is to be announced.

" Anything that sounds hard and means nothing."

Why are you so cheerful?
Do you think you have cause to know sorrow?

The fellow made me walk about three feet high.

Closed brains.

DIE IRLEN: (Prague, Bohemia.)
     (Translation by Roy Temple House.)

          At last he dies in that shrill plastered cell -
          He dies again, who died long years before,
          Like the young fruit that rotted round the core,
          But clung a time and withered, ere it fell.
          Who knows what tales the ashy lips could tell
          Had they but spoken when the dull eyes wore
          A dreamy ecstasy that comes no more,
          Or his ears beat to some far battle swell?
          His life was like a bell whose tone is thin
          And false and broken, since the fatal day
          When the brute casters riveled at the inn.
          Now all the dissonance has died away:
          His ear is careless of the mad-house din,
          His dust is quiet, and his soul is gay.

     France, the laboratory of freedom.

Like Brand I will not compromise but unlike him this applies to
myself as well as to the others. I will live out my life as it is
giving in neither way in order to gain success. I will rather be
true to life than to any ideal or rather I will make life the ideal.
To be specific: I will not give up a wife, I will not give up children
for the sake of art let us say. That were a compromise in respect of
life. It is a compromise to acknowledge an incapacity to know and live
through all in contreal, to hold marriage in abeyance.
  This is the answer to Brand in this formula.

Go dump your pail of wonder in the Rhine."
              (With captions such as this group the fragments.)

                  An old woman, who was mad
                  Lives in her house
                  With two starry children!
                  Who are nothing to her.
                  In and out run cats and their
                      Young about her.

    (Print these tatters in small er type.)

    The red shadow of a large ear on a pink neck.

    Your beauty has become to me -
    God knows what your beauty has become to me -
              Torture perhaps !

Cold is very disagreeable but it's clean. When you are hot you are
dirty.

    I have no fault to find with life except that it is utterly contempt
able.
    The clouds we almost reach when the winds lull.

Leipzig! Leipzig! Where the grass is swept with brooms
And roses bloom until December in the public parks!

Hark Hilha! Heptachordaan hymns
Invoke the year's initial ides!
Like liquid lute's low languishing
Dim dawn defeated dusk derides!
Awake for at aurora's advent angel anthemnings arise!

Give me the roar of the tempest. The storm blast
That roots the great forests and spreads the white
Foam like a cloud
O'er the mountainous rocks of the ocean
Give me the power to sin
With an imbenent hell at my elbow
With the king of all hate for a foe
Oh give me the glory of battle,
The bitterness bred of defeat
And the fierceness of joy in the conquest.
Let women bask still in perfumes
With afeminine God for a father
But thou my stern Master I pray
Give me Hell for reward if I fail
And a vict'ry o'er death if I concuer.

Bright locked and cheeyful mid the stormy morn.

As sturdy a horse-godmother as ever drank from a keg.

My life is but a travesty and scandle on myself. I have lived to belie
my nature, all men do; all men are better than this disguise which grows
about and stifles them.   Copy?

Oh God, could I but wake a fiery master to my doubts, a passion in me
stronger than my fears.

A laugh ho! Laugh for the lady. Nay that's a smile; set it to music,
vocalize it.

H.Kuanst, 1573. 5 vols. on the divine, noble gift, the philosophical,
highly dear and wondrous art of making beer.

Fiume.

Her eyes are as blue light through the tips of waves;
Her voice is as the call of the waves,
Soft, entreating;
Loud, compelling;
Like the sound of waves
Deriding music of crude measure.
Her touch is of the life of foam
Where the spirit lifts in passion
For the waves clash and lag and meet
And fall contending
No less than is the motion of her spirit,
With the white touch borne outward
Which is sleep in the hollows
Upon the burthening blue level of our nights and days.

Die Weiber von Weimberg. (Carrying men on their shoulders, as now.)

Castle at Al Modovar. Bet. Sevilla and Cordova.

Her mood changed as at Gibraltar the water changes from blue to green.

Gibraltar -

She moved through them like a blue current in a green ocean.

            Wonderful creatures!
            Why must I call you Bride and Mother?
            Curse on the idle mockery and fashion lie of such names.
            Be delight unto me rather,
            Joy at the encounter,
            Sorrow at the ends of things,
            Be to me deeds of compassion;
            Have these for name, none other.

Peculiar as a sea-wise chicken.

Suggestion for you: Two oxen could not or imagined they could not pull a
waggon up a hill. Another yoke of oxen was put in front of them and started
unhitched. The first two pulled the load up easily.
    " Christian Science" so called is a noteable criticism on our state of
mind, we are the first pair of oxen.

And then we looked and ached and parted
Lost all for gain
Our whole pleasure has merely been
A delayed God-speeding
Yet time is infinite.

There are people who laugh at the serious things in life and forget that th
the serious things are the funniest of all.
All seriousness is a form of humor.

Wonderful ruin at Warburg, Westphalia.

Wilhelm Kalf. Remarkable brass urn at Hague.

Wonderful! The greatest writer that ever writ a rote..

Thought I have slept with. Men have so looked upon this breasted creature,
so loved her rounded limbs, her long hair and features that they have not
usually paused to look at her , to consider and wonder: Here am I yet there
is a new thing, an entire creation like myself yet entirely different, a
whole destiny between, in the interchange the eternal flow between our dis-
similarities I may live quickened.

early

Sometimes when I could envy them their mirth
Who're young and live their lives out carelessly,
I have seen them often by the quiet sea
Waist deep, in clinging stuffs little of girth
That shadow whole youth's slender tracery,
Youth whom I feign with dark eyes and brown hair,
When I see well how far better it were
To cease than half live with full life so nigh
Then flames my Ladie's Spirit on whose birth
My heart so weighs, with promises which fear
Dares call no thing for breathing how she'll wear
One day all youths: Skies, sea's, earth

        From Ymir's flesh
        The earth was shaped.
        And from his brain
        Were all the gloomy
        Clouds created.   Griminsmal.

Antwerp.   Hotel La Vielle Tour. Aug. 4, '09.
Youth is by right fickle; This is the very birthright of true strength.
For youth loves all then how can it ignore all but all that ie loves to
make itself almost a hermit in affection by being constant. It knows little
It is all eyes but blind yearnings, then let it be so, let it yearn for the
truth as it will. Trust it, respect it and above all let it not lean over-
much on supports or better do not bolster and prop where there is no need
for supportfor then it revolts at your lie and lack of faith and leaps
away an disgust from your blindness.

Modern Invocation.

Rise in the air with a roar of wings spirits,
Muses of all nations, Greek,Chinese, French,
English, Spanish, all; and you my own
For you are spirits and have no bodies,
Nor do you die. Then let the old be met
Midway in air by the new between earth
And the twenty mile deep surface where breath ends.
Join over woods streatching like dry billows,
Seas, cities with smoke and red houses
And sing of the modern young man
Journeying to freedom, sing!
Sing of the hell of modern desire
That cannot go on ships as Odyssus the Greek hero did
But must tear up the monotony of indolence
And voyage in it's own heart. Sing of heroism
That languishes silently for a lover;
Sing of the new
Sing of the here! Sing loudly!
Also sing with beauty not always sweet!
Sing of pain and the terror of ignorance!
Commerce you must praise
Praise gigantic enterprises!
For lo! I stand here listening by morning and evening,
In my own land with heaped up daisies in my arms
Which I hold up to you as offering and sign
That i will hear and interpret you
In letters to my people that they may have joy.
Let birds be your messengers,
Let swallows and the yellow warbler talk shrill
In the trees of your songs that i may hear.

ILLINOIS POETRY SERIES

Laurence Lieberman, Editor

NATIONAL POETRY SERIES

So Often the Pitcher Goes to Water
until It Breaks
Rigoberto González (1999)
Selected by Ai

Manderley
Rebecca Wolff (2001)
Selected by Robert Pinsky

Renunciation
Corey Marks (2000)
Selected by Philip Levine

OTHER POETRY VOLUMES

Local Men and *Domains*
James Whitehead (1987)

Her Soul beneath the Bone: Women's
Poetry on Breast Cancer
Edited by Leatrice Lifshitz (1988)

Days from a Dream Almanac
Dennis Tedlock (1990)

Working Classics: Poems on
Industrial Life
*Edited by Peter Oresick and Nicholas
Coles* (1990)

Hummers, Knucklers, and Slow
Curves: Contemporary Baseball
Poems
Edited by Don Johnson (1991)

The Double Reckoning of
Christopher Columbus
Barbara Helfgott Hyett (1992)

Selected Poems
Jean Garrigue (1992)

New and Selected Poems, 1962–92
Laurence Lieberman (1993)

The Dig and *Hotel Fiesta*
Lynn Emanuel (1994)

For a Living: The Poetry of Work
*Edited by Nicholas Coles and Peter
Oresick* (1995)

The Tracks We Leave: Poems on
Endangered Wildlife of North
America
Barbara Helfgott Hyett (1996)

Peasants Wake for Fellini's *Casanova*
and Other Poems
*Andrea Zanzotto; edited and
translated by John P. Welle and Ruth
Feldman; drawings by Federico Fellini
and Augusto Murer* (1997)

Moon in a Mason Jar and *What My
Father Believed*
Robert Wrigley (1997)

The Wild Card: Selected Poems,
Early and Late
*Karl Shapiro; edited by Stanley Kunitz
and David Ignatow* (1998)

Turtle, Swan and *Bethlehem in Broad
Daylight*
Mark Doty (2000)

Illinois Voices: An Anthology of
Twentieth-Century Poetry
*Edited by Kevin Stein and G. E.
Murray* (2001)

On a Wing of the Sun
Jim Barnes (3-volume reissue, 2001)

Poems
*William Carlos Williams; introduction
by Virginia M. Wright-Peterson* (2002)

The University of Illinois Press
is a founding member of the
Association of American University Presses.

Composed in 10/14 ITC Galliard
with Gill Sans display
by Jim Proefrock
at the University of Illinois Press
Designed by Dennis Roberts
Manufactured by Thomson-Shore, Inc.

University of Illinois Press
1325 South Oak Street
Champaign, IL 61820-6903
www.press.uillinois.edu